A Tad Overweight, but
Violet Eyes to Die For

Doonesbury books by G. B. Trudeau

Still a Few Bugs in the System
The President Is a Lot Smarter Than You Think
But This War Had Such Promise
Call Me When You Find America
Guilty, Guilty, Guilty!
"What Do We Have for the Witnesses, Johnnie?"
Dare To Be Great, Ms. Caucus
Wouldn't a Gremlin Have Been More Sensible?
"Speaking of Inalienable Rights, Amy . . ."
You're Never Too Old for Nuts and Berries
An Especially Tricky People
As the Kid Goes for Broke
Stalking the Perfect Tan
"Any Grooming Hints for Your Fans, Rollie?"
But the Pension Fund Was Just Sitting There
We're Not Out of the Woods Yet
A Tad Overweight, but Violet Eyes to Die For

In Large Format

The Doonesbury Chronicles
Doonesbury's Greatest Hits

a Doonesbury book by

GB Trudeau.

A Tad Overweight, but Violet Eyes to Die For

Holt, Rinehart and Winston
New York

Published by Holt, Rinehart and Winston,
383 Madison Avenue,
New York, New York 10017.

Published simultaneously in Canada by Holt, Rinehart and
Winston of Canada, Limited.

Library of Congress Catalog Card Number: 79-3443

ISBN: 0-03-049186-X

First Edition

Printed in the United States of America

The cartoons in this book have appeared in newspapers
in the United States and abroad under the auspices of
Universal Press Syndicate.

2 4 6 8 10 9 7 5 3 1

THE LIBERAL CULT. HUMANE. JUST. FREE-SPENDING. AND UNDER THE GUIDANCE OF ITS CHARISMATIC LEADER, "TED", A MYSTERIOUS NEW FORCE ON THE POLITICAL SCENE!

WHO ARE THESE "LIBERALS"? HOW CAN WE ACCOUNT FOR THEIR CURIOUS APPEARANCE IN AN ERA OF FISCAL RESPONSIBILITY? WE ASKED CONSERVATIVE COLUMNIST DIRK DUPONT.

BEATS ME. I THOUGHT WE HAD THE SUCKERS UNDER CONTROL.

COMING UP: A LIBERAL'S MOTHER RECALLS HER SHAME.

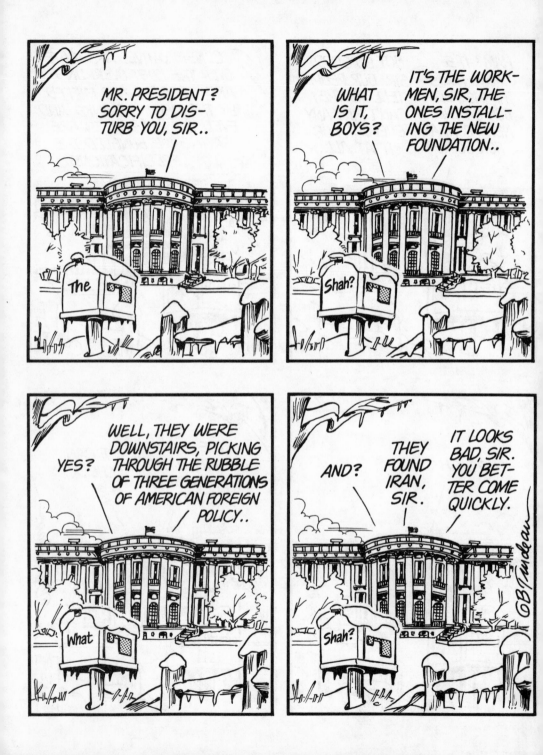

DAY, MAY 8, 1979
Californian Creates 'Context' For White House Bid
Vows Commitment To Public Mood
By Rick Redfern
SACRAMENTO, California, May 7 – Today, in a press ference at
THE WAS
Carter Symbol Chief to Defect
Cardigans Seen in Sacramento
By Rick Redfe
WASHINGTON May 7 – The Phonathon, Tree House Fireside said he w
Secretary of Symbolism Duane Delacourt
THE CAPITOL
5-8
THE WAS
Campaign '80:
Brown Assembles 'Mellow Mafia'
Tom Hayden, Others, to Sell Out
Analysis by Rick Redfern
Governor Jerry Brown is sometimes compared to a Rorschach test; people see in him what they want. How else to explain
buzz words buzz words buzz words
MY, HAVEN'T WE BEEN A BUSY BOY!
WE NEED THE MONEY.
GBTrudeau

FLIGHT 81, ARRIVING 3:30 P.M... OKAY, I GOT IT.
WHAT'S THE NEW HOUSE LIKE, HONEY?
RUSH
YOU'RE GOING TO LOVE IT, SHEILA. IT'S A LITTLE CONDO ONLY 200 YARDS FROM THE BEACH. IT WAS THE FIRST ONE I LOOKED AT.
RUSH
HAVE YOU SEEN ANY CALIFOR-NIANS YET?
JUST THE NEIGH-BORS.
A REAL RUSH
ANYONE OFFERED TO SHARE HIS SPACE YET?
NOT AT THESE PRICES. BUT WE DO GET SUNDECK PRIVILEGES.
REALLY
GB Trudeau